The Raaga Cookbook – Modern Indian Cuisi.
Fresh Flavors Redefined

Photography by Douglas Merriam
www.douglasmerriam.com

Edited by Margo Chan Taylor

ISBN-13 978-1507672358
ISNB-10 1507672357

TABLE OF CONTENTS

ACKNOWLEDGEMENTS

TO

My Mother,
Raj Rani Rawal, Super Cook

and

My Father,
Commander Dayal Das Rawal
whose extraordinary belief has made this possible

My special thanks to my friends, colleagues, guests at Raaga, and the Community of Santa Fe for their support.

The many Chefs and Managers during my early tenure with the Sheraton group of Hotels, and the Leela group of Hotels.

I would also like to express my thanks to Doug Merriam for the wonderful photos in the book. And, special thanks to Margo Chan Taylor, who served as my editor, for so quickly showing faith in the possibilities of this book.

Last, but not least, Chef Johnny Vee for agreeing to write the foreword.

My very special gratitude to Abigail Davidson for being there for me, as an ever present support.

FOREWORD

America's love affair with the exotic flavors of India is deliciously evident in the continued popularity of this taste-bursting cuisine. At Paddy's Raaga in Santa Fe, New Mexico, Chef Paddy Rawal has been wowing the palates of locals and visitors alike with his creative take on classic dishes, as well as his ultra-inspired original creations. Now fans of the seemingly mysterious blend of spices and ingredients can recreate many of the scrumptious dishes that have made Raaga one of the City Different's most beloved eateries. The book starts with a mini-cooking class describing the elements of flavor and techniques you will need to produce an authentic Indian feast. You will feel as though Paddy were standing over you gently guiding you as you combine garlic, ginger, cumin, turmeric, and so much more to build the unique flavor profile. This cookbook goes way beyond the curry dishes you remember and takes you on a journey into regional Indian cookery. Raaga means "sweet melody"; in this must-have cookbook, you will discover that each recipe is a tune deliciously sung.

Chef Johnny Vee
Director, Las Cosas Cooking School

PREFACE

This book is a celebration of the best in Indian Cooking, exemplified by the menu served at Raaga - Modern Indian Cuisine, in Santa Fe, New Mexico.

Over the last 30 years, it has been my privilege to observe and learn from my late mother and to work with some of the best known names in Indian Cooking.

The recipes in this book are not the usual restaurant fare, where it is not unusual to sacrifice the palate to please the eye. The delicacies, though exotic, are easy-to-make and a veritable home cook's delight.

My food is "Spicy" not "Chilli Hot." I like to say "Spiced for flavor, not for heat." We make use of our exotic spices for their special flavor and aroma. The use of red or green chillies is at one's own discretion. The recipes in this book are "Light" and "Spicy."

Indians come from different regions, religions, and castes. They, of course, do share a common ethos with one another's cuisine, in a limited way. They share similar methods of slow-cooking and ingredients in common, particularly spices. But their knowledge of other cuisines is usually limited to those communities where they have friends and visit their homes for a meal. In any city in India there are several communities, including religion and caste communities. At weddings where guests run into the hundreds, the cooking is done by special wedding caterers and each community has their own. And this sector is a repository of culinary secrets as much as in the home where cuisine is taken seriously.

To the uninitiated, Indian cooking seems like a jigsaw puzzle incapable of a solution. The reason is simple: there is no recorded text for Indian Cuisine. Every *Genre* of cooking has innumerable schools, each school more than one style, each style its own *Guru*.

Recipes are handed down from generation to generation, but never recorded - only memorized. As a consequence, every recipe is open to interpretation, but there is no standard recipe at all.

WHY AN INDIAN MEAL?

It is first and foremost carbohydrate-dominated, with emphasis on wheat *rotis* and rice as a staple food. Unlike pasta, Indian *Roti* is a whole wheat bread, retaining the entire goodness of the grain.

Vegetables play a more dominant role in Indian cuisine. Usually, one green, and one other vegetable, form part of every meal.

Protein is also present in the Indian diet, of course, but much more effort is made to use protein derived from lentils and dairy products, rather than meat. Legumes or dal (lentils) boiled with herbs and tomatoes, seasoned with spices and eaten with rice, provide amino-acid that constitutes a "complete protein". Meat and Fish are eaten too, but in smaller quantities.

Yogurt is important because it introduces good flora into the digestive system. A vegetarian meal inclines towards being alkaline which is much better for health than an acidic one.

WHAT EXACTLY IS CURRY?

Curry, as the word is used today in India, and around the world, simply means gravy or sauce. In a way, Indian cuisine is like classical Indian music, or Raaga. It has been handed down through generations without a written code. So curries, like other dishes, have always lent themselves to improvisation. And since there are no rigid or classic recipes for any curry dish - any number of good cooks would have a different recipe for the same dish – one really has to search for the best tasting recipe for a dish.

Contrary to common belief, not all Indian dishes are curries. However, "curry" has become a catch-all name for any spice-based meat or vegetable dish with a sauce. Curries can be watery, dry, red, yellow, green, hot, or really, really hot- it is completely up to the chef or household. A standard food called curry does not exist. A curry could be vegetarian or non-vegetarian. It could be coconut infused, or bitter with asafetida, also called "hing." It could be cooked with yogurt or with cashew nuts.

RESOURCES

Savory Spice Shop – Santa Fe
225 Galisteo St, Santa Fe, NM 87501
Phone: (505) 819-5659

Talin Market World Food Fare
505 Cerrillos Rd Suite B-101, Santa Fe, NM 87501
Phone: (505) 780-5073

INTRODUCTION

Growing up in India has had its fascinations, but almost nothing can equal a child's memory of meals partaken in the kitchen of granny's home. Across the cool of mornings would echo the hooves of cattle let out to graze after they had been drained of their morning's supply of milk. As cauldrons of milk would be set on wood fed stoves, the women of the house (most rural homes believe in joint families) would bustle around churning buttermilk, adding dollops of butter to the previous night's leftover *rotis* or unleavened breads.

Because my father served in the Indian Navy, we traveled all over India, and so began a journey that was linked by memorable repasts and feasts, parties and meals enjoyed in different homes, with different flavors. How different a *dal* or lentil curry could be in Southern India with its vegetables from those cooked in Western India, which was sweetened with *jaggery*. Or a dish of beef or lamb or chicken or fish, cooked in fat and chillies in Goa, curried in coconut in coastal India, tenderized with pomegranate in Hyderabad, or with papaya in Northern India, cooked with potatoes in Lucknow as stew, or pounded into a paste and garnished with raisins and almonds in Kashmir. Or take rice, eaten steamed or cooked with lemon yogurt, or made appetizing with the addition of peas, or turned into a *Biryani* flavored with lamb or chicken, and garnished with saffron, and as a *Kheer* or porridge with cashew nuts and raisins and pistachios as India's simplest, but most popular dessert.

Not that this is a simple process, for the food habits of Indians are as complicated as their rituals and beliefs. More than half the nation is vegetarian due to religious beliefs. But just as the Brahmins or priests, shun meat, so do the Kshatriyas or warriors extol its values. The Muslims eat beef, but not pork, but the Hindus - those who are not vegetarian - eat pork, but not beef. Some meat-eating communities do not eat fish for it is considered dirty, while other vegetarians do not mind fish, calling it a "vegetable of the sea," because it is cold blooded. Yet others do not eat bright colored vegetables, such as carrots or tomatoes, for they are supposed to excite passion, and for that very reason, the Jain community will not include onions and garlic in their diet.

Typically, an Indian meal begins with a glass of buttermilk, fresh lime soda, or even a soup served with a *pappadum*. The main course consists of rice or *rotis* or both, eaten with servings of vegetables, dal, chicken or lamb curry, and yogurt. Accompaniments include a variety of pickles and chutneys, as well as salad. The meal is not served in courses, but all together, so the diner can savor different flavors simultaneously: sour, bitter, salty, sweet, pungent, spicy, and hot. Chai (tea) is served at the very end of the meal. It is considered the finale to the Indian meal.

The strongest influence on Indian Cuisine or at least 80 percent of Indians - the Hindus - is Ayurveda, an ancient body of knowledge on health. Ayurveda is not confined to medicine only: it covers the whole subject of life in its various ramifications. It discusses the purpose of life, the importance of mental as well as physical health, and a code of ethical conduct for healthy living.

Ayurveda understands the properties and actions of food differently from Western science. The bio-chemistry of an edible product is not everything. For example, vegetable oil and dairy fat, such as *ghee* (clarified butter) from cow's milk, are not seen merely as fats, but in terms of their effect on the body. Ghee is cooling, while oil heats the body.

BEVERAGES

TENDER COCONUT SHIKANJI (Fresh Ginger blended tender coconut water with a touch of lemon)

Serves 4
Preparation time: 30 minutes

Ingredients

4 Green Tender Coconuts – these may be purchased at Talin Market
3 Lemons, juiced
5 oz. Powdered Sugar
1 TBS Ginger Juice

Method

Extract the water from the coconuts; scrape the cream from the sides of the coconut.
Blend with the coconut water.
Chill in a refrigerator for 20 minutes.
Dissolve the sugar in the coconut water.
Add juice of 3 lemons and ginger. Strain.
Pour into serving glasses.

FRESH SQUEEZED LEMON JUICE

Serves 4
Preparation time: 15 minutes

Ingredients

6 Fresh and Firm Lemons
¼ tsp White Pepper Powder
3 TBS Powdered Sugar
1 tsp Black Salt
8 – 12 oz. Club Soda, Ginger Ale or Water

Method

Squeeze juice from the lemons into a pitcher. Add sugar/salt/white pepper.
Use a whisk and vigorously mix the ingredients.
Pour in glasses. Add the Club Soda/ Ginger Ale/ Water. Mix again
Taste for sweetness, serve.

MASALA BUTTERMILK (Thin Consistency Yogurt)

Serves 4
Preparation time: 15 minutes

Ingredients

1 - 2" piece Fresh Ginger Root
1 small White Onion
1 tsp Whole Cumin seed
1 tsp Fresh Cilantro
1 TBS Black Salt
1 tsp Chaat Masala
32 oz. tub Plain Yogurt
16 oz. Water

Method

Peel the onion, chop finely, set aside.
Peel and clean the ginger root, chop finely, set aside.
Toast the cumin seeds in a skillet, until it gives out the aroma, set aside (watch carefully, as they can burn easily!).
Wash and finely chop the fresh cilantro, set aside.
Chaat Masala, preferably 'Shaan' brand from grocery store.
Yogurt, your choice, non-fat, low fat.....
In a bowl or pitcher, add the onion, ginger root, cilantro, salt, chaat masala, cumin.
In another bowl, whip the yogurt with a whisk, add the water.
Mix the ingredients of both the bowls, taste for seasonings and serve.

MANGO LASSI

Serves 4 Preparation Time: 15 minutes

Ingredients

32 oz. Plain Yogurt
32 oz. can Mango Pulp
4 TBS Sugar
10 oz. Water
1 tsp Ground Cardamom

Method

Place all ingredients in a bowl, except ground cardamom. Whisk enough to blend all ingredients
Serve with a sprinkle of ground cardamom on top.

RASAM

Serves 4
Preparation time: 30-40 minutes, cooking time: 40 minutes

Ingredients

1 cup Lentils (Masoor dal)
2 tsp Ginger, chopped
2 TBS Tamarind Juice
1 tsp Black Peppercorn, crushed
½ tsp Asafetida (Hing)
1 TBS Salt
¼ tsp Turmeric powder
2 pints Water

For Tempering

1 tsp Coriander Powder
6 Roma Tomatoes, chopped
½ tsp Black Mustard seeds
1 tsp Cumin seeds, crushed
1 tsp White Sesame seeds
1 ½ tsp Garlic, chopped
1 sprig Fresh Curry Leaves

Method

Soak the tamarind in warm water for 5 minutes, squeeze out the juice and discard the root.
Soak the lentils in water for ½ hour. Liquefy in a blender.
Heat the Tamarind extract in a pot. Add the turmeric powder, salt, coriander powder and tomatoes.
Cook on low heat for 20 minutes.
Add the cumin, garlic, ginger, peppercorns and asafetida. Cook for another 10 minutes.
Stir in the lentils along with the water. Bring to a boil, reduce heat and cook for 10 minutes.
Remove from heat, strain.
For the Tempering, heat oil in a pan, add mustard seeds, curry leaves. Sauté until you hear them crackle.
Add to the lentils. Stir and Serve.

INDIAN CHAI

Chai recipes are like Italian minestrone soup – it's always good, but everyone's recipe is different.

[FOR ONE PERSON]

One cup water
1 Cinnamon Stick
1 tsp Fennel seeds
4 ea Cloves

¼ cup Milk
3 pods Green Cardamom
1" piece of fresh Ginger Root
3 tsp Tea Leaves

1. Set the water to boil, add all the spices.
2. Once the water comes to a boil, add the milk, let it cook for 3-4 minutes.
3. Add the tea leaves, let the liquid brew. The tea leaves have to brew enough to release the taste and flavor, not just the color.
4. Strain and serve.

STARTERS

LASOONI GOBHI (Cauliflower florets in a tomato garlic sauce)
Serves 6
Preparation time: 30 minutes, cooking time: 15 minutes

Ingredients

1 head Cauliflower
1 tsp Ginger Paste
8 TBS Tempura Batter
1 tsp Salt
3 TBS Ketchup

1 tsp Garlic Paste
4 tsp Corn Starch
½ tsp White Pepper
1 - 12 oz. can Tomato Sauce
2 TBS Garlic, chopped

Method

CAULIFLOWER:
Cut the Cauliflower into medium size florets. Boil for 5 minutes, until al dente.
In a mixing bowl, add the tempura batter, corn starch, ginger paste, garlic paste, salt, white pepper. Add water and mix, until you get a thick batter consistency.
Dip the florets in the batter, fry lightly. Set aside.

SAUCE:
Heat 2 tsp of oil in a skillet Add the garlic and lightly fry until golden brown. Add a tsp of sugar, tomato sauce, ketchup. Cook for 5 minutes.

FINISH:
Heat a skillet on medium heat, pour in the sauce, let it come to a boil, add the cauliflower florets, toss for a minute. Serve.

STUFFED POBLANO PEPPER

Ingredients

1 Small Poblano Pepper
1 TBS Onion, chopped
1 tsp Garam Masala
1 tsp Ginger Garlic paste
6 TBS Gram Flour
Salt to taste

1 Boiled potato
1 tsp Cumin seeds, toasted
1 tsp Chaat Masala
2 TBS Cooked Yellow Lentil
1 tsp Baking Powder
Oil for frying

Method

Mix the Gram flour and baking powder, add water to form a thick and silky paste. Set aside.

Crush the potatoes to a mush, add the onions, ginger, fenugreek, cumin, garam masala, chaat masala, garlic ginger paste, cooked yellow lentils. Mix well together.

Char grill the Poblano so as to easily peel the outer skin, slit the Poblano on one side, deseed.

Stuff them with the mixture.

Dip them in the gram flour batter.

Heat oil in a pot on medium heat. Fry until golden brown.

Serve.

LENTIL KABAB (Spiced Lentil Cutlets)

Serves 4
Preparation time 30 minutes, Cooking Time 15 minutes

Ingredients

1 cup Lentils (Masoor Dal)/1 cup Chana Dal
1 tsp Green Chillies, chopped
1 TBS Cilantro, chopped
2 tsp Ginger, chopped
Salt

Pinch Red Chilli Powder
4 TBS Breadcrumbs
1 TBS Corn Starch
1 tsp Garam Masala
1 Red Onion, chopped

Method

Clean, wash and boil the lentils, adding a pinch of salt while boiling, for 15 minutes or until cooked.
In a mixing bowl, add the lentils, onion, green chillies, garam masala, cilantro, ginger, salt to taste, red chili powder, bread crumbs, and cornstarch. Mix well.
Divide the mixture into 16 portions and shape into flat coin shaped discs.
Heat frying oil in a pot. Deep fry the kababs until golden brown on the outside.
Remove and serve with Ketchup, Hot Sauce, or Soy Ginger Sauce.

HARA KABAB (Shallow Fried Medallions of Spinach and Green Peas)

Serves 4
Preparation time: 30 minutes, cooking time: 20 minutes

Ingredients

1 lb. Green Peas, boiled
1 TBS Garam Masala
1 tsp Green Chillies, chopped
6 TBS Bread Crumbs
Vegetable Oil for frying

2 Bunches Spinach, boiled
1 tsp Chaat Masala
1 TBS Ginger, chopped
3 TBS Corn Starch

Method

Put the spinach and peas in a blender, until coarsely blended.
Add the rest of the ingredients to the mixture, mix well in a mixing bowl, by hand.
Divide into equal portions and shape into squares, rounds or hearts, per your liking.
Heat oil in a large nonstick skillet. Bring to medium heat and start frying in small quantities.
Turn the kababs after two minutes of frying on first side, and fry the other side.
Serve with Mango chutney or Garlic Mustard Aioli.

VEGETABLE PAKORAS

Ingredients

1 large Russet Potato
1 Zucchini
1 Eggplant
3.5 oz. Gram Flour
2 tsp Cornstarch
1 Fresh Ginger Root

1 large bunch Fresh Spinach
1 Yellow Squash
1 Red Onion
1 tsp Cumin seeds
2 TBS Coriander seeds
Oil for frying

Method

Wash and finely slice the vegetables in thin julienne. Then finely dice them. Set aside.
Skin Ginger and finely grind. Add to the vegetables in a bowl.
Add the salt for taste, green chillies if you want a kick and coriander and cumin seeds.
Add the Gram flour and cornstarch.
Add water, a little bit at a time to emulsify the ingredients and coat the flour.
Form little balls with the mixture.
Heat oil in a pot and fry until cooked. Medium heat will get the pakoras cooked in the inside and out.
Serve.

CHILLI POPPERS

Ingredients

6 Serrano Chillies
2 TBS Onion, chopped
1 tsp Garam Masala
1 tsp Ginger Garlic paste
6 TBS Gram Flour
Oil for frying

1 Potato, boiled
1 tsp Cumin seeds, toasted
1 tsp Chaat Masala
1 TBS Fenugreek Leaves
1 tsp Baking Powder

Method

Mix the Gram flour and baking powder, add water to form a thick and silky paste. Set aside.
Crush the potatoes to a mush, add the onions, ginger, cumin, garam masala, chaat masala, garlic ginger paste, fenugreek leaves. Mix well together.
Slit the serrano on one side, deseed.
Stuff them with the mixture.
Dip them in the gram flour batter.
Heat oil in a pot on medium heat. Fry until golden brown.
Serve.

CHICKEN SATAY

Ingredients

1 boneless, skinless Chicken Breast
1 TBS Coconut Powder
3 TBS Coconut Milk
Vegetable Oil for frying

1 tsp Ginger Paste
1 TBS Peanut Butter
3 oz. Heavy Cream

Method

Wash and clean the chicken breast thoroughly.
Using a knife, slice the chicken into thin slivers or nuggets. Pound them with the bevel of the knife to flatten them.
Sprinkle the coconut powder and salt on both sides of the chicken. Place in a bowl.
After 5 minutes, add the ginger paste to the chicken. Mix well.
Heat oil in a nonstick skillet.
Lightly fry the chicken nuggets 2 minutes on one side, then flip.
One minute after the flip, add the coconut milk, heavy cream and peanut butter.
Cook until sauce thickens.
Serve.

SPINACH CHAAT

Ingredients

3 oz. Fresh baby spinach leaves
2 tsp Tomatoes, chopped
Red Chilli powder
Sweetened Yogurt
Water

2 tsp Onions, chopped
Black Salt
Tamarind Sauce
2 TBS Chick Pea Flour
Oil for frying

Method

1. Add 1 TBS of water to the chick pea flour, mix thoroughly and set aside.
2. Add the spinach to the flour mixture, coat the leaves thoroughly.
3. Heat the frying oil to high heat.
4. Drop the spinach in the oil and keep tossing and turning in the oil with a sieve.
5. Remove within ½ minute of frying.
6. Sprinkle a pinch of black salt, red chilli powder.
7. Drizzle the tamarind and sweetened yogurt.
8. Top with chopped onions and tomatoes.
9. Serve immediately when warm.

S O U P S

TOMATO AND FENNEL SOUP
Serves 4
Preparation time: 15 minutes, cooking time: 30 minutes

Ingredients

8 Roma Tomatoes, chopped
½ tsp Fennel Powder
1/3 tsp Ground White Pepper
2 tsp Garlic, chopped
2 tsp Butter

1 tsp Cumin seeds
2 TBS Onions, chopped
3 Bay Leaves
6 cups Vegetable Stock
3 TBS Oil

Method

Heat the oil in a pot, turn to medium heat. Add the Cumin seeds. When they begin to crackle, add the onions, garlic, bay leaves, fennel powder. Add the garlic, tomatoes, salt, white pepper, vegetable stock. Allow to simmer for 20 minutes.
Remove from heat and let it cool.
Blend to obtain a puree, strain with a fine strainer and reheat.
Transfer to soup bowls and serve.

CHICKEN AND SPINACH SOUP

Ingredients

6 oz. Cooked Chicken Breast
2 TBS Onions, chopped
1 tsp Garlic, chopped
1 tsp Lemon Juice
7 cups Chicken Stock
Oil

1 ½ cups Fresh Spinach, chopped
1 tsp Cumin seeds
2 tsp Ginger, chopped
1/3 tsp Ground White Pepper

Method

Heat oil in a pot. Bring to medium heat. Add the onions, cumin seeds, sauté for 2 minutes.
Slice the chicken, add to the pot. Add the ginger, garlic and sauté for 2 minutes.
Add the spinach, sauté for 1 minute. Add the white pepper powder, chicken stock, lemon juice.
Serve.

LENTIL AND COCONUT SOUP

Ingredients

1/2 cup Yellow Lentils
3 TBS Onions, chopped
1 tsp Ginger, chopped
1 tsp Lemon Juice

5 Curry Leaves
2 tsp Coconut Powder
8 cups Vegetable Stock

1 cup Red Lentils
1 tsp Cumin seeds
1 tsp Garlic, chopped
1/3 tsp Ground White Pepper
½ tsp Turmeric
1 cup Coconut Milk
½ tsp Green Onions, chopped

Method

Boil the lentils for 10 minutes, until fully cooked. Add the turmeric and stir. Put aside.
Heat oil in a pot, turn to medium heat.
Add the onions, sauté for 2 minutes, add the cumin, garlic, ginger, curry leaves.
Add the white pepper powder, lemon juice, vegetable stock, simmer for 5 minutes. Add the lentils. Salt, to taste.
Add the coconut milk, simmer for another 5 minutes.
Serve in a bowl, with a pinch of coconut powder and chopped green onions.

CARROT AND ORANGE SOUP - Pureed Carrot blended with orange juice, served hot

Serves 4
Preparation time: 1 hour, cooking time: 40 minutes

Ingredients

2 ½ cups Carrots, diced
1/3 tsp Ground White Pepper
3 oz. Sugar
½ cup Heavy Cream

1 TBS Ginger, chopped
4 cups Orange Juice
4 oz. Butter
½ cup Onion, chopped

Method

Heat the butter in a skillet. Add the onions and sauté for 2 minutes.
Add the carrots, sauté for 2 minutes. Add the remaining ingredients, except the cream.
Cook on low heat until the carrots are tender.
Remove and pass thru a soup strainer.
Reheat the strained soup and stir in the cream. Transfer to soup bowls.

COLD CUCUMBER SOUP - Cucumber blended with cream, served chilled

Serves 4
Preparation time 30 minutes, cooking time 45 minutes

Ingredients

6 English Cucumbers, diced with skin
4 oz. Butter
1/3 cup Onions, chopped
8 cups Vegetable Stock

½ tsp Toasted Cumin seeds
1/3 tsp Ground White Pepper
½ cup Heavy Cream

Method

Heat the butter in a pot. Add the onions and sauté for 2 minutes, add the cumin.
Add the cucumbers, sauté for a few minutes
Stir in the vegetable stock, salt to taste, white pepper powder. Cover and cook on low heat for 20 minutes. Stir in the cream.
Allow to cool.
Blend the soup in a blender, strain if needed once again.
Place in the refrigerator until chilled. Serve.

SALADS

CHICKEN AND MINT SALAD
Serves 4
Preparation time: 20 minutes

Ingredients
½ lb. Chicken, cooked
7 oz. Garbanzo Beans, cooked
1 Cucumber, diced
1 TBS Mango Chutney
2 tsp Fresh Mint, chopped
1 bag Salad Greens

1 lb. Red Cabbage, shredded
2 tsp Chaat Masala
1 can (7 oz.) Diced Tomato

Method
Cooked chicken may be boiled or grilled.
Mix all the ingredients except the salad greens, in a mixing bowl. Ensure that the ingredients are blended evenly. Chill in refrigerator.
Portion the salad greens in four serving bowls and top it with the rest of the mixture from the mixing bowl. Serve.

INDIAN HARVEST

Serves 4
Preparation time: 20 minutes

Ingredients

3.5 oz. Green Peas
7 oz. Heart of Palm, drained
6 oz. Paneer, cubed

3.5 oz. Flour Chips (see below)
1 Avocado, diced
1 bag Baby Spinach

Method

Wash and drain the first three ingredients.

For the Chips: Knead a handful of wheat flour dough with the addition of water only. Let it sit for 5 minutes. Roll it into a sheet. Using a pizza cutter make small diamond shaped pieces.
Heat oil in a skillet, fry the chips. Let them cool.
Boil the Paneer for 5 minutes in water, add a pinch of turmeric and salt to the water. Cool.
Mix all the ingredients except the baby spinach, in a mixing bowl. Use any dressing that suits you. Italian......
Portion and serve the finished salad on a bed of baby spinach.

TOMATO TAMARIND

Serves 4
Preparation time: 40 minutes

Ingredients

8 Roma Tomatoes, firm
Flour Chips or Corn Chips
6 TBS Tamarind Sauce

1 bag Baby Arugula
3.5 oz. Spicy Cashews, roasted
3 TBS Balsamic Vinegar

Method

Wash the baby arugula, rinse and chill in the refrigerator
Quarter the tomatoes, sprinkle with a little salt and chill separately.

For the Tamarind Sauce: 2 oz. of *Jaggery*, 1 packet of seedless tamarind (Indian or Thai), 2 tsp of roasted cumin, 10 dates (optional).
Boil all the above ingredients for the sauce in a pot, until thoroughly cooked and it forms a thick concentrate.
Strain through a colander or strainer. Let it cool.
Add balsamic vinegar, stir vigorously.
Portion out the arugula on plates, top with tomatoes, cashews and chips.
Serve with the tamarind dressing.

EGGPLANT SALAD WITH POMEGRANATE SEEDS AND EXTRA VIRGIN OLIVE OIL

Serves 4

Preparation Time: 10-15 minutes, cooking time: 10-15 minutes

Ingredients

1 large Indian Eggplant
1 oz. Extra Virgin Olive Oil
1 cup Yogurt
Salt, to taste
1 TBS Fresh Ginger, chopped
8 Fresh Mint Leaves

3 TBS Pomegranate seeds
2 oz. Olive Oil
3 tsp Yellow Mustard
White Pepper, to taste
2 TBS Honey

Method

Heat 1 ½ oz. olive oil a non-stick pan.

Cut eggplant into thin slices and shallow fry in the hot oil till golden brown. Drain on absorbent paper.

Put yogurt, mustard paste, salt, white pepper powder and ginger in a bowl and mix well. Add honey and 1 oz. extra virgin olive oil and mix well. Put it in the freezer for 5 minutes.

Finely chop mint leaves. Arrange a few eggplant slices in a bowl. Spread half the yogurt mixture on them. Place the remaining eggplant slices over the yogurt. Sprinkle half the mint leaves and 2 TBS pomegranate seeds. Spread the remaining yogurt mixture once again and add remaining pomegranate seeds. Sprinkle remaining mint leaves and 1 oz. olive oil and serve.

MOTH AND MOONG SPROUT SALAD

Ingredients

¾ cup Sprouted Moth Beans

¾ cup Sprouted Green Moong Beans

1 medium Red Onion, chopped

1 medium Green Bell Pepper

1 medium Roma Tomatoes, diced

1 small Thai Green Chilli

2 tsp Lemon Juice

1 tsp Chaat Masala

Salt, to taste

1 TBS Green Onions, chopped

Method

Mix the sprouted moth and moong, onion, bell pepper, tomato and green chilli in a bowl.

Cover with cling film and refrigerate for half an hour.

For the dressing: mix together the lemon juice, chaat masala and salt. Add the dressing to the chilled salad just before serving. Garnish with green onions and serve at once.

ENTREES

TANDOORI CHICKEN

The king of Kebabs, Tandoori Chicken is the best known Indian delicacy and the tastiest way to barbeque chicken.

Serves 4
Preparation Time: 2 hours, cooking time: 15 minutes

Ingredients

1 - 2 lb. Chicken
4 TBS Lemon Juice
6 oz. Heavy Cream
2 ½ tsp Garlic Paste
½ tsp Garam Masala
2 TBS Gram Flour

Salt
8 oz. Yogurt
2 ½ tsp Ginger Paste
1 tsp Cumin Powder
1 tsp Saffron
Butter, for basting

Method

The Chicken: Clean, make deep incisions - 3 on each breast, 3 on each thigh, 2 on drumstick. Make a paste of salt, lemon juice and rub over the chicken evenly. Put aside for 15 minutes.
The Marinade: Whisk yogurt in a large bowl, add the remaining ingredients and mix well. Rub the chicken with this mixture. Put aside for 1 hour.
Preheat oven to 350°F.
Place the chicken in a roasting pan and cook for 10 minutes. Baste with melted butter and cook again for 5 minutes.

TANDOORI CHICKEN

METHI CHICKEN

As with almost every delicacy, Methi (Fenugreek) Chicken tastes best with fresh fenugreek. Dried fenugreek is also available as a spice.

Ingredients

1 ½ lbs. Chicken, cut up in cubes
Salt
Whole Spices: 1 tsp Cardamom/5 Cloves/1 Cinnamon Stick/8 Black Peppercorns
1 ¾ cups Onion, chopped
5 TBS Ginger
½ tsp Turmeric
1 cup Tomatoes
1 cup Fresh Spinach

8 oz. Yogurt
5 oz. Ghee
3 TBS Garlic
1 tsp Green Chillies
1 tsp Ground Coriander
4 TBS Fresh Fenugreek
6 oz. Chicken Stock

Method

The Chicken: Clean and wash the chicken cubes and set aside.
The Marinade: Whisk the yogurt, add the salt, mix the chicken in this and leave in refrigerator for 30 minutes.
The Vegetables: Cut, chop and dice the onions, tomatoes, garlic, ginger and green chillies.
Cooking:
Heat the ghee in a large pot, add the whole spices and sauté on medium heat until they crackle. Add the onions and sauté until golden brown. Add the garlic, ginger and green chilies, stir for 2 minutes.
Add turmeric and coriander powder- dissolved in 2 oz. of warm water, stir for 3 minutes.
Add the tomatoes and sauté until the fat starts separating from the mixture.
Add the chicken and the entire contents of the marinade. In addition, add chicken stock.
Bring to a boil, cover and simmer until the chicken is fully cooked.

MATTAR PANEER

A Chef's original vegetarian delight.

Serves 6
Preparation Time: 1 hour, cooking time: 30 min

Ingredients

For Paneer (Cheese)
3/4 lb. Paneer
1 tsp Saffron
1/4 cup Milk
3 oz. Corn Starch

2 Green Chillies
1 TBS Ginger
Salt

For Sauce

¼ cup Ghee
2 TBS Ginger Paste
1 ½ tsp Garlic Paste
2 Green Chillies
4 oz. Tomato Puree
3 TBS Ground Cashews
1 TBS Garam Masala

1/3 cup Boiled
Onion Paste
1 tsp Ground
Coriander
1 cup Yogurt
¼ cup Heavy Cream

The Paneer: Grate the paneer in a bowl, finely chop the green chillies, ginger and mix into the paneer.
Boil the milk with the saffron, divide in two parts.
Add half the milk to the paneer mix.
Make little balls of the paneer mix, dust with corn starch.
Heat oil in a skillet and fry the paneer balls.
The Sauce: Whisk the yogurt, ginger and green chillies. Set aside.

Method

Heat the ghee in a pot, add the onion paste and garlic paste. Cook for 3 minutes on medium heat.
Add the ginger and green chillies and cook for another 3 minutes.
Add the coriander and garam masala and cook until the ghee separates.
Add the tomato puree, bring to a boil and simmer for another 5 minutes.
Add the yogurt, with the remaining milk, add the cashew, and cream.
Reduce to medium heat and cook until consistency of the sauce is silky and smooth.
Add the green peas and paneer balls and cook for 3 minutes.

LAMB VINDALOO

Serves 4
Preparation time: 40 min, cooking time: 45 min

Ingredients

1 ½ lbs Boneless Lamb
½ cup Red Onion, chopped
Salt

7 oz. Olive Oil
3 Potatoes, quartered

The Marinade:
½ TBS Rice Vinegar
1 TBS Sugar
8 Cloves

1 tsp Crushed Black Pepper
8 Green Cardamom Pods
3 Whole Green Chillies

The Sauce:
6 Whole Red Chillies
1 tsp Cumin seeds
¼ tsp Turmeric
2 TBS Ginger

8 sticks Cinnamon
4 tsp Coriander seeds
1 TBS Garlic
5 cups Water, Chicken
or Beef Stock

The Lamb: Wash and clean lamb. Cut into 1" cubes.
The Vegetables: Chop Onions, fry the potatoes in oil and set aside.
The Marinade: Grind the Red chilies in a blender. In a bowl, mix the other ingredients and let the lamb sit in it for an hour.
The Sauce: Peel and chop the garlic, chop the ginger. Put the remaining ingredients of the sauce in a blender and liquefy.

Method

Heat oil in a pan, add the onions and sauté on medium heat until golden brown. Add the sauce and cook until smooth.
Add the lamb and sauté for 5 minutes. Add water or stock, bring to a boil, cover and simmer until lamb is tender, about 30 minutes. Add the potatoes.

PATRANI FISH

A weight watcher's dream. A Parsi delicacy.

Serves 4
Preparation Time: 40 minutes, cooking time: 30 minutes

Ingredients

1 ¾ lb. White Fish
Banana Leaves
2 TBS Mustard Oil

6 TBS Rice Vinegar
Salt
3 Lemons

COCONUT CHUTNEY

1 ¼ cup grated coconut powder
1 TBS Chilies
3 Oz. Ground Coriander
4 TBS Lemon Juice
1 Bunch Fresh Mint

1 Bunch Cilantro
2 Bulbs Garlic
2 Oz. Ground Cumin
Salt
2 tsp Sugar

Method

The Fish: Wash and pat the fillets dry, cut each fillet into two. Make horizontal slits in the pieces to create pockets. Dust with salt and vinegar and set aside for 20 minutes.
The Banana Leaf: Trim, wash and wipe dry.
The Chutney: Chop the mint, cilantro leaves, green chillies, and garlic. Put all these ingredients and the coconut powder in a blender and make a paste.
The Wrapping: Stuff the pockets in the fish with the paste, spread the rest on both side of the fillet. Apply oil on the banana leaves and place the fillet on it. Wrap each fillet in the leaves.
Cooking: Steam the fish in a double boiler or a skillet with water and a plate above it immersed and then a lid to create steam for about 30 minutes.

SHRIMP KORMA

A Blend of Moghlai and Nawabi Cuisine.

Serves 6

Preparation Time 1 hour, Cooking Time 30 min

Originally this dish was made with almonds only, however, nowadays in modern cooking, we tend to use a combination of cashews and almonds.

Ingredients

1 ½ tsp Poppy seeds
5 oz. full fat Yogurt
2 ½ oz. Ghee
2 oz. Almonds, blanched
2 oz. unsalted Cashew Nuts
1 Cinnamon Leaf
12 oz. Onions, chopped
2 tsp Garam Masala
½ tsp Nutmeg, ground

1 lb. Raw Shrimp
3 tsp of Garlic Paste
2 tsp Coriander seeds
2 tsp Carrom seeds
4 oz. Ginger Paste
2 Jalapeno, chopped
1 ½ tsp Kasoori Methi
4 oz. Heavy Cream
½ tsp Mace powder

1. Soak the poppy seeds in 2/3 cup of water for 1 hour. Then drain and grind to a paste.
2. Hang the yogurt in a cheese cloth, until fully drained of whey. Then whisk in a bowl.
3. Heat the ghee in a cooking pot, reserving one tablespoon. Add the almonds, cashews and cinnamon leaf. Fry for 7-8 minutes over moderate heat. Add the onions and fry for another 10 minutes until translucent.
4. Add the jalapeno, poppy seeds and sauté for 3 minutes. Add 7 oz. of water and cook for 10 minutes. Remove from heat, discard the bay leaf and leave to cool. Put the mixture in the blender and puree to a smooth paste.
5. Add the reserved ghee to another cooking pot , add garlic, ginger. Sauté for 1 minute, add the shrimp. After 3 minutes, add the yogurt and stir constantly, so as to prevent it from curdling. Add heavy cream and simmer for 2 minutes.
6. Add the ground spice mixture, nutmeg, mace and salt. Add 8 oz. warm water or vegetable stock. Cook till the sauce is of a thick viscosity.

SHRIMP KORMA

RICE PREPARATIONS

CHICKEN BIRYANI

Serves 6
Preparation Time: 45 minutes, cooking time: 45 minutes

Ingredients

2 lbs. Chicken Breast
½ cup Ghee
2 Black Cardamom Pods
2 Sticks Cinnamon
2 tsp Black Cumin seeds
4 tsp each Ginger and Garlic Paste
1 tsp Saffron
1/2 cup Fresh Mint

2 ½ cups Basmati Rice
6 Green Cardamom Pods
6 Cloves
2 Bay Leaves
1 cup Onion
2 ½ cups Yogurt
2 TBS Milk

Method

THE CHICKEN: Wash, clean and pat dry the chicken cubes. Set aside
THE RICE: Wash in running water and soak in a utensil for 30 minutes. Add salt, half of the whole spices. Place on the gas stove and bring to a boil. Cook until the rice is almost done.
THE VEGETABLES: Finely slice the onions and finely chop the mint.
THE YOGURT: Whisk in a bowl and divide into two equal portions. Set aside.
THE SAFFRON: Dissolve in warm milk. Add half to one portion of the yogurt. Set aside other half.
Pre-Heat oven to 375 ° F

COOKING
Heat the ghee in a pot, add the remaining whole spices, sauté until the cumin seeds crackle Add the onions, and sauté till golden brown.
Add the ginger and garlic paste, stir for 1 minute. Add the chicken and cook for 4 minutes.
Add the plain yogurt, and 7 oz. of water. Bring to a boil and then simmer until the chicken is almost done, but not fully cooked, about 20 minutes.
In another pot, place the chicken, make layers of saffron yogurt, mint and rice, twice.
Place a moist cloth on top and place in the oven for 15 minutes.
Serve from the bottom of the pot, include both the chicken and rice.

LEMON RICE

Serves 4
Preparation Time: 20 minutes, cooking time: 20 minutes

1 cup Basmati Rice	8 Cashew Nuts
1/4 tsp Ground Turmeric	Salt
3 TBS Oil	2 TBS Onions, chopped
1/8 tsp Black Mustard Seeds	10 Curry Leaves
1 TBS Lemon Juice	2 TBS Yogurt

Grated Coconut Powder or unsweetened Desiccated Coconut Powder

Method

Wash the rice in running cold water.
Soak the cashew in 7 oz. of water for 10 to 15 minutes.
In a pot, add the rice and add 1 ½ cups water. Bring to a boil.
When boiling, add turmeric and salt.
About 11 minutes later, when all the liquid is absorbed and the rice is cooked, turn off the heat.
Remove the rice and spread out in a flat dish. Leave for 20 minutes.
In a large skillet, heat the oil. Add the onions, mustard seeds, curry leaves and fry until the mustard seeds crackle.
Add the lemon juice, yogurt and rice. Stir well to incorporate all the ingredients evenly.
Sprinkle with grated coconut powder and serve.

LAMB BIRYANI

Serves 4
Preparation time: 30 minutes, cooking time: 1 hour 30 minutes

Ingredients

1 lb. Lamb, cubed
1 lb. Basmati Rice
3 pints Water
1 tsp ea. Black, Green Cardamom Pods
Pinch Saffron
4 Bay Leaves
3 tsp Biryani Masala

3 oz. Onions, chopped
5 tsp Ginger-Garlic Paste
3 TBS Onion Paste, browned
Salt, to taste
6 Cloves
3 oz. Onions, chopped, browned
Water

Method

Soak the rice for 30 minutes
Heat 1 ½ pints of water in a pot until it comes to a boil. Add the rice, cardamom, clove and bay leaves.
Cook the rice about 12 minutes, until almost done. Set aside.
Heat oil in a pan, add the onions and sauté until brown in color. Add ginger-garlic paste and sauté for another minute.
Add the lamb pieces and biryani masala and cook for 10 minutes. Add salt and 1.5 pint water and cover. Cook for another 20 minutes on low heat.
Remove the lid, add the brown onion paste (see below for process) and continue cooking till the lamb is tender, about 20 minutes.
In a casserole, place alternate layers of rice and lamb. Sprinkle with saffron.
Pre heat the oven to 375° F.
Put casserole in oven for about 10 minutes.
Remove and serve.
For Brown Onion Paste:
Slice 1/2 pound of onions and fry over medium heat until brown. Remove, drain excess oil and cool. Process in a blender until pulped.

SHRIMP BIRYANI

Serves 4
Preparation time: 1 hour, cooking time: 25 minutes.

Ingredients

3.5 oz. Shrimps, shelled
3/4 lb. Basmati Rice
14 oz. Water
Salt, to taste
Pinch Turmeric
3 tsp Vegetable Oil
2 Black Cardamom pods

4 Cloves
4 Bay leaves
1 medium Onion, sliced
2 tsp Ginger-Garlic paste
1.5 pints Vegetable Stock
4 Green Cardamom pods
2 oz. Milk

Method

Soak the rice for 30 minutes.
Boil the water in a pot, add turmeric, lemon juice, salt, shrimps. Remove when cooked, about 7 minutes.
Heat oil in a pot, add the whole spices, let them crackle. Add the sliced onions, sauté until golden brown. Add the ginger-garlic paste and sauté until the paste is dissolved. Add the vegetable stock and bring to a boil. Add the butter, and lemon juice. Add the rice and cook over medium heat, stirring occasionally.
When the stock has cooked down to the level of rice, add the milk and shrimps and cover with a muslin cloth.
Cook over low heat for 15 minutes. Transfer to a serving dish and serve.

VEGETABLE BIRYANI

Serves 6
Preparation Time: 45 minutes, cooking time: 30 minutes

Ingredients

2 cups Basmati Rice

1/3 cup Sliced Almonds
4 TBS Raisins
Whole Garam Masala - 6 ea. Cardamom Pods/2 Black Cardamom Pods/6 Cloves/2 Sticks Cinnamon/2 Bay Leaves/Pinch of Red Mace
Salt
3 TBS Ginger
¼ tsp Turmeric
1 tsp Saffron
1/3 cup Fresh Mint, chopped

½ lb. Frozen Vegetable Blend
1/3 cup Cashews
1/3 cup Ghee

1 large Yellow Onion
1 ½ TBS Garlic
1 cup Yogurt
1 oz. Milk
Water

Preparation

The Rice: Wash and drain under running cold water. Soak in a pot for 30 minutes, then drain.
In the pot, add 2 cups of water, bring to a boil, turn heat down to medium, set aside when water has evaporated, about 17 minutes.
The Vegetables: Rinse and par boil the vegetables, strain and set aside.
The Yogurt: Whisk in a bowl and divide in two portions.
The Saffron: Dissolve in warm milk. Add half to one portion of the yogurt. Set aside other half.
The Oven: Pre-heat to 375°F.

Method

Heat the ghee in a pot. Add the remaining garam masala and sauté over medium heat until it begins to crackle. Add the onions, sauté until golden brown.
Add the vegetables and stir for 2 minutes.
Add the portion of plain yogurt, stir and add 1 cup of vegetable stock, bring to a boil, then simmer until the vegetables are cooked.
Add the dry fruits, adjust the seasoning.
Sprinkle half each of the saffron yogurt, mint on top.
Spread half of the rice over the vegetables.
Sprinkle the remaining saffron yogurt, mint and rice as another layer.
Place a moist cloth over the rice, cover with a lid.
Put the pan in the oven and cook for 15 minutes.

VEGETABLE BIRYANI

BREADS AND CHUTNEYS

NAAN
Serves 8
Preparation Time: 2.5 hours, cooking time: 15 minutes

Ingredients

2 lbs. Flour
1 cup Water
3 tsp Salt
1 ½ tsp Baking powder

2 cups Milk
½ cup Yogurt
2 TBS Sugar
4 tsp Oil

Method

Mix flour, salt, yogurt, sugar, baking powder. Add the water and milk. Knead into a soft and smooth dough. Add oil, and knead the dough vigorously, cover with a moist muslin cloth. Set aside.
After 2 hours, when the dough has proofed, divide the dough in 8 equal portion balls, then place on a lightly dusted baking tray.
Flatten each ball, roll fine with a rolling pin.
Heat the oven to 425° F.
Place the uncooked bread on a lightly oiled baking sheet and bake in the oven for two minutes.

STUFFED POTATO PARANTHA

Serves 8
Preparation Time: 45 minutes, cooking time: 12 minutes

Ingredients

1 lb. Wheat Flour
3 Potatoes, boiled and grated
2 TBS Cilantro, chopped
2 TBS Onion, chopped

2 ½ cups Water
1 tsp Salt
1 TBS Ginger, chopped
Oil

Method

Sift the flour in a mixing bowl. Add the water and knead the dough to a soft and smooth texture.
Set aside for 30 minutes.
In a separate bowl, add the potatoes, ginger, onions, salt, cilantro and mix well. Portion the dough into 8 balls.
Take each ball, flatten, add the potato mixture. Refold and flatten with a rolling pin.
On a gas stove, heat a nonstick skillet, turn heat to medium.
Lightly oil the skillet, place the flattened dough and cook. Turn after the first side is golden brown and repeat the process for the other side.

CHUTNEYS

GREEN CHUTNEY

Preparation Time: 20 minutes

Ingredients

1 cup Mint Leaves
2 cups Fresh Cilantro
1 large Jalapeño
½ small Red Onion

1/4 tsp Salt
1 tsp Sugar
1 TBS Lemon Juice

Method

Using a blender, puree all the ingredients to a fine, silky consistency.

COCONUT CHUTNEY

Preparation Time: 20 minutes

Ingredients

4 oz. Coconut, grated
1 small Red Onion, chopped
2 tsp Cilantro, chopped
½ tsp Salt
2 tsp Lemon Juice
6 Dates, pitted

1 clove Garlic
¼ tsp Cumin powder
1 tsp Sugar
3 TBS Tomato Ketchup
1 TBS Ginger, chopped

Method

Using a blender, puree all the ingredients to a fine, silky consistency.

DESSERTS

SHAHI TUKRA

Serves 6
Preparation Time: 30 minutes, cooking time: 30 minutes

Ingredients

12 oz. Ricotta Cheese
3 cups Sugar
2 cups Water
½ tsp Green Cardamom powder
12 Slices bread

Vegetable Oil for frying
½ gallon Whole Milk
2 TBS Almonds, sliced
2 tsp Pistachio
1 tsp Saffron

Method

The Syrup: Boil the sugar with the water to make a simple syrup; add cardamom powder and stir. Set aside.
The Bread: Slice off the outer crust and trim the edges to make circular discs. Heat the oil and fry till light golden.
The Milk: Bring to a boil in a pot, remove one ounce for the saffron and set aside.
The Tukra: Immerse the fried bread in the remaining milk, the slices at least an inch apart. Return the pan to the fire and cook until the milk is absorbed. Turn each slice at least once during the procedure. Remove from heat and pour the syrup over.
The Dry Fruits: Sprinkle over the bread.
The Saffron: Dissolve in the milk, set aside, stir while it is still warm. Pour over the bread.

KULFI (Indian Ice Cream)

Serves 8
Preparation Time: 45 minutes

Ingredients

4 TBS Sugar
1 – 29 oz. can Mango Pulp
1 - 14 oz. can Evaporated Milk
1 quart Heavy Cream

Method

Add the sugar and milk in a heavy bottomed pot, cook for 10 minutes over low heat. Mix well and leave to cool.
Stir in the cream and the mango pulp.
Use a mold or 5 oz. containers with lids. Fill with the kulfi and set in the freezer prior to serving.

GULAB JAMUN

Makes 30
Preparation Time: 1 hour, cooking time: 20 minutes

Ingredients

14 oz. Bisquick
8 oz. Powdered Milk
6 TBS Flour
½ tsp Baking Soda
4 cups Sugar

2 cups Water
6 Green Cardamom Pods
2 drops Rosewater
6 TBS Flour
Vegetable Oil for frying

Method

The Mixture: Mix the Bisquick, powdered milk, flour and baking soda in a mixing bowl.
Knead gently by adding a little milk. Make 30 small balls of equal size.
The syrup: Boil the sugar with the water to make a simple syrup.
The cooking: Heat oil and deep fry the balls until dark golden brown. During the frying,
swirl the oil and pour over each ball, until the ball floats to the top. Remove and immerse
immediately in the syrup.

PHIRNI (Rice Conde)

Serves 10
Preparation Time: 1 hour

Ingredients

4 cups Milk
¼ cup Basmati Rice
1 ¼ cup Sugar
1 tsp Saffron
4 tsp Almond Slivers

1 tsp Ground Green Cardamom
2 drops Rosewater
2 tsp Pistachios

Method

The Rice: Wash in running cold water. Soak in water for 30 minutes. Drain, put in blender, add 2 tsp water and blend to a fine paste.
The Saffron: Dissolve in 1 oz. of warm milk. Set aside.
The Nuts: Mix and chop.
Boil the remaining milk in a pot, add the rice paste and sugar, while stirring continuously with a whisk. Reduce to low heat and continue cooking, until the mixture reaches a custard consistency. Add the dry fruits, saffron and rosewater.
Distribute the Phirni in ramekins and set aside in the refrigerator to cool before serving.

APPENDIX

GARAM MASALA
6 oz. Cumin seeds
2 oz. Coriander seeds
1 oz. Black Cardamom Pods
1 oz. Green Cardamom Pods
1 oz. Black Peppercorns
1 oz. Ginger Powder
10 1" Sticks Cinnamon
3/4 Oz. Cloves
1/4 Oz. Mace
1 Whole Nutmeg

Put all the ingredients in a spice grinder and grind to a fine powder. Store in a sterilized, dry, airtight container.

GARAM MASALA II
3 oz. Cumin seeds
2 oz. Black Cardamom Pods
2 oz. Black Peppercorns
2 oz. Green Cardamom Pods
1 oz. Coriander seeds
1 oz. Fennel seeds
½ oz. Cloves
10 1" Sticks Cinnamon
½ oz. Bay Leaves
3 Whole Nutmeg
½ oz. Ginger Powder

Put all the ingredients, except the ginger powder, in a spice grinder and grind to a fine powder. Transfer to bowl, add the ginger powder, mix well. Store in a dry, airtight container.

ONION PASTE
2 ¼ lbs. Yellow Onions
3 Bay Leaves
3 Black Cardamom Pods
1 cup Water

Peel, wash and chop the onions. Place in a pot. Add the bay leaves, Cardamom and 1 cup of water. Bring to a boil, simmer until onions are translucent. Liquefy in a blender.

GINGER PASTE
The Ginger: Peel or Scrape, wash and chop coarsely 1 cup of Ginger Root.
The Paste: Place 3 oz. of water and the chopped ginger in a blender and make a fine paste. Remove and refrigerate. It will be good for 3 days.

GARLIC PASTE
Peel and smash 1 cup of Garlic cloves.
Place the garlic in a blender. Add 3 oz. water and blend to a fine paste. Refrigerate. It will be good for 3 days.

CASHEW PASTE
Soak 1 cup whole cashews in warm water for 30 minutes. Drain the cashews, add 3 oz. of water, place in a blender, make a fine paste. Refrigerate. It will be good for 36 hours.

TAMARIND PULP
Tamarind is a fruit that grows on a tree. The fruit is the pulp within the shell. Remove the pulp from the shell or purchase tamarind in pulp form. Soak a 2 oz. piece in warm water for 30 minutes. Squeeze as much juice out as much as possible. Discard the rest.

Made in the USA
Middletown, DE
28 November 2017